From Seed to Maple Tree

Following the Life Cycle

by Laura Purdie Salas   illustrated by Jeff Yesh

PICTURE WINDOW BOOKS
Minneapolis, Minnesota

Thanks to our advisers for their expertise:

Kathryn Orvis, Ph.D., Associate Professor/Extension Specialist
Department of Youth Development & Agricultural Education
Purdue University, West Lafayette, Indiana

Terry Flaherty, Ph.D., Professor of English
Minnesota State University, Mankato

Editor: Shelly Lyons
Designers: Nathan Gassman and Lori Bye
Page Production: Melissa Kes
Associate Managing Editor: Christianne Jones
The illustrations in this book were created digitally.

Picture Window Books
151 Good Counsel Drive
P.O. Box 669
Mankato, MN 56002-0669
877-845-8392
www.picturewindowbooks.com

Photo Credits: © iStockphoto/VinceLi, 23.

All books published by Picture Window Books
are manufactured with paper containing at least
10 percent post-consumer waste.

Library of Congress Cataloging-in-Publication Data
Salas, Laura Purdie.
From seed to maple tree : following the life cycle / by Laura Purdie Salas ;
illustrated by Jeff Yesh.
p. cm. — (Amazing science: life cycle)
Includes index.
ISBN 978-1-4048-4931-0 (library binding)
1. Maple—Life cycles—Juvenile literature. I. Yesh, Jeff, 1971- ill. II. Title.
QK495.A17S25 2009
583'.78—dc22   2008006438

Table of Contents

Tree Life Cycles

Like animals, trees and other plants have a life cycle. There are many kinds of trees. Let's look at the life cycle of a sugar maple tree. We will see how it changes over seasons and years.

Maple trees are deciduous. This means they lose their leaves each year.

A Seed in Spring

Trees start out as seeds. Even the largest tree grows from a tiny seed. Sugar maple seeds lie on the ground at the end of winter. The days get longer. The snow melts. Then it is time for a seed to germinate, or sprout.

Giant redwood trees can grow to be more than 300 feet (91.5 meters) tall. Their trunks can be 30 feet (9.2 m) wide. But even they start out from very small seeds.

A Seedling

A strong white root pushes out of the sugar maple seed and into the ground.

A stem grows upward through the soil and into the air.

The seed grows into a small plant. The young plant is called a seedling. Sunlight and water help the seedling grow strong.

Sugar maple seedlings are a favorite food for white-tailed deer.

Growing Tall and Strong

Each year, the seedling grows during spring and summer. The sun and warm temperatures during those two seasons help the tree grow. The tree grows about 1 foot (.3 m) taller each year. Its trunk gets a little thicker.

The seedling becomes a sapling when it reaches a height of more than 6.6 feet (2 m). Growth continues for about 30 to 40 years. Then the maple tree is an adult. Its growth slows down.

Sugar maples can stand 70 to 110 feet (21 to 34 m) tall. They can live 300 to 400 years.

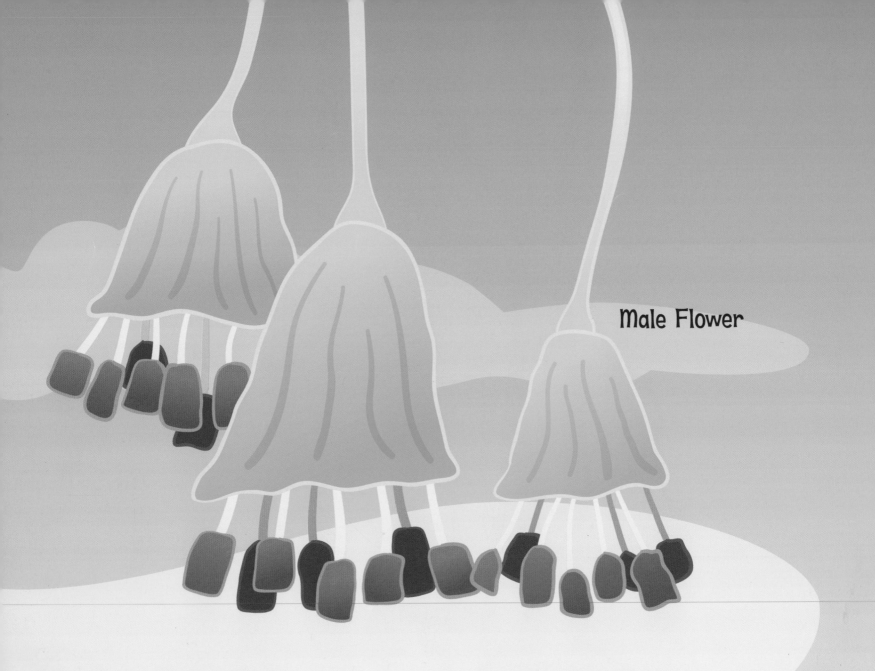

Male Flower

Flowers Make Eggs

An adult sugar maple tree grows flowers in spring. The flowers are greenish-yellow and droopy. Each flower can have both male and female parts. But it can also have just male or just female parts. The male parts make a yellow powder called pollen. The female parts make eggs.

Female Flower

When a sugar maple tree is flowering, the tree looks yellow.

From Flowers to Fruit

Wind and insects help make new maple trees. A good wind can pick up the pollen and blow it onto another maple tree's flower. Bees and other insects can carry pollen, too. The pollen lands on the female part of a flower. This process is called pollination.

14

Bees help with pollination. A bee stops at a sugar maple flower to drink its liquid, or nectar. Pollen on the flower sticks to the bee's feet. The bee flies to another flower. This time, its feet leave the pollen behind.

The Fruit

A pollinated sugar maple flower grows into a fruit. The hard fruit is called a double samara. It looks like a pair of seeds with small wings attached.

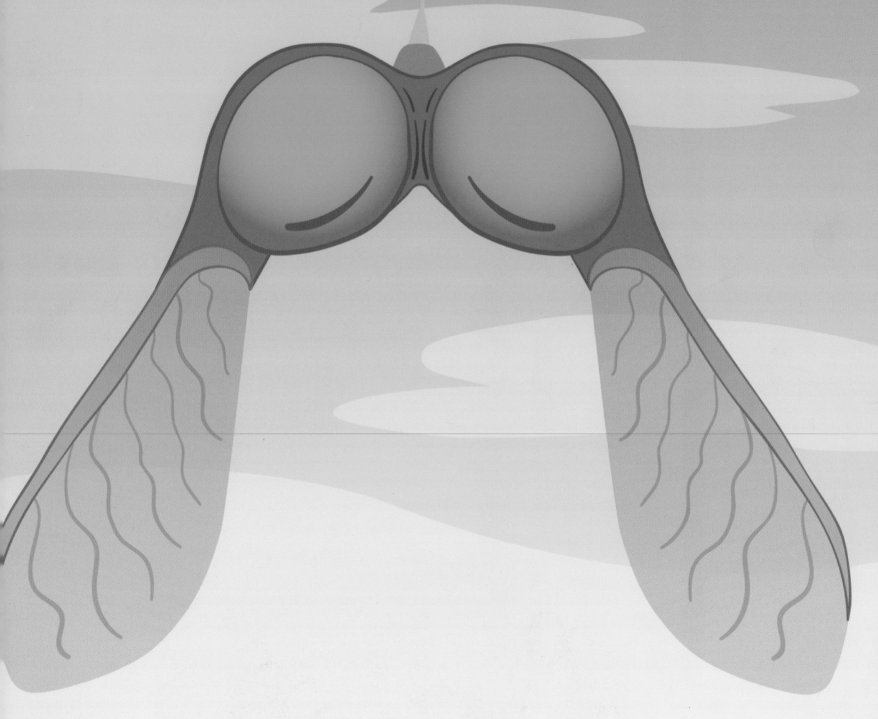

The fruit ripens in September or October. Then it falls from the tree. Usually the fruit carries one seed inside. The seed will be able to grow into a sugar maple tree.

In fall, it is good for seeds to be covered by leaves on the ground. The leaves hide the seeds from squirrels, birds, and other seed-eating animals.

17

Flying Seeds

The winged shape of the double samara helps the fruit catch the wind. The fruit can blow far away from the parent tree.

The parent tree uses lots of water and food from the soil. Because of this fact, seeds grow better when they are not near their parent tree. Seeds also need to be cold and wet during winter. These conditions help them sprout during the next spring.

Leaves get their green color from chlorophyll. During fall, there is less sunlight for leaves to absorb, so they start breaking down the chlorophyll for energy. Then the leaves change into bright colors. Soon the leaves will fall to the ground.

Wintering

During winter, the double samara lies on the ground. It does not break open. The seed does not start to grow. But inside the seed is still alive and preparing for spring.

20

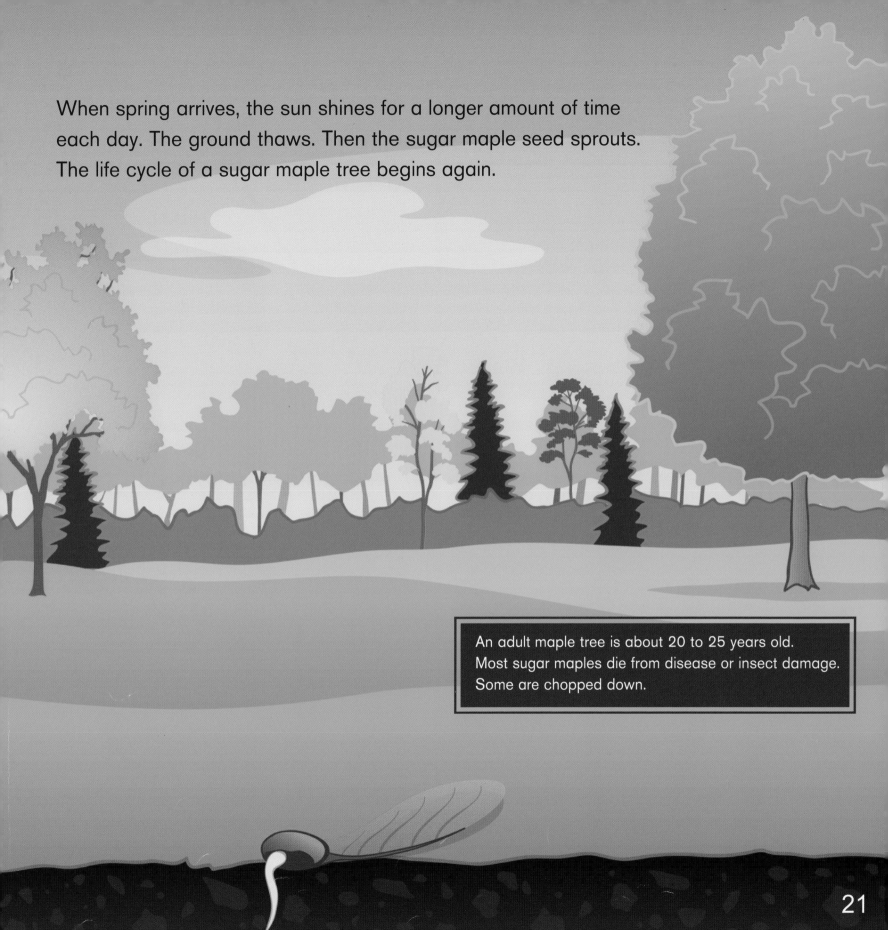

When spring arrives, the sun shines for a longer amount of time each day. The ground thaws. Then the sugar maple seed sprouts. The life cycle of a sugar maple tree begins again.

An adult maple tree is about 20 to 25 years old. Most sugar maples die from disease or insect damage. Some are chopped down.

Life Cycle of a Sugar Maple Tree

1. Seed
5-6 months

2. Seedling
1-15 years

3. Sapling
16-30 years

4. Adult Maple
30-195+ years

Fun Facts

- Sugar maples in forests grow straight and tall. But sugar maples grown in the open branch out near the ground and spread out.

- When people carve initials or words in a tree, it is like making a cut on your arm. Germs can enter the tree through the open cuts in the bark.

- Maple syrup comes from the sugar maple tree. People make syrup from the sap, or sugary water, that flows inside the tree each spring.

- Many things in a tree's surroundings will affect its growth. The amount of sun and water, the temperature, and the quality of the soil are just a few things that will either speed up or slow down a tree's growth. Because these things will be different from year to year, the length of time each tree spends in each stage of growth may also differ greatly.

Adult sugar maple tree

Glossary

chlorophyll—dark green cells in leaves

deciduous—a type of tree with leaves that fall off

fruit—a product of plant growth

germinate—when a seed sends out a root and a stem

pollen—a powder made by flowers to help them create new seeds

pollination—the process of a female part of the flower receiving pollen

roots—the part of a plant that grows underground and soaks up water and nutrients

double samara—a dry, usually one-seeded winged fruit

sapling—a young tree that is taller than 6.6 feet (2 m) and has a trunk that is less than 4 inches (10 centimeters) around

seed—part of a flower that will grow into a new plant

seedling—a young tree that is about 6 to 80 inches (15 to 200 cm) tall and has a trunk that is less than 4 inches (10 cm) around

To Learn More

More Books to Read

Fowler, Allan. *Maple Trees.* New York: Children's Press, 2001.

Kalman, Bobbie, and Kathryn Smithyman. *The Life Cycle of a Tree.* New York: Crabtree Pub. Co., 2002.

Marshall, Pam. *From Tree to Paper.* Minneapolis: Lerner Publications Co., 2003.

Thoennes Keller, Kristin. *From Maple Trees to Maple Syrup.* Minneapolis: Capstone Press, 2005.

On the Web

FactHound offers a safe, fun way to find Web sites related to topics in this book. All of the sites on FactHound have been researched by our staff.

1. Visit *www.facthound.com*
2. Type in this special code: 1404849319
3. Click on the FETCH IT button.

Your trusty FactHound will fetch the best sites for you!

Index

Look for all of the books in the Amazing Science: Life Cycles series:

From Caterpillar to Butterfly: Following the Life Cycle
From Mealworm to Beetle: Following the Life Cycle
From Puppy to Dog: Following the Life Cycle
From Seed to Daisy: Following the Life Cycle
From Seed to Maple Tree: Following the Life Cycle
From Tadpole to Frog: Following the Life Cycle